GW00675191

U.S. AIR FORCE
39714

NG
2283
NAVY
602

VIETNAM WARBIRDS IN ACTION

DANA BELL

ARMS AND ARMOUR PRESS
London New York Sydney

First published in 1982, 1983 and 1984 as *Air War over Vietnam*, vols I, II and IV.
First published in this combined edition in 1986 by Arms and Armour Press Limited, 2–6 Hampstead High Street, London NW3 1QQ.

Distributed in the USA by Sterling Publishing Co. Inc., 2 Park Avenue, New York, N.Y. 10016.

Distributed in Australia by Capricorn Link (Australia) Pty. Ltd., P.O. Box 665, Lane Cove, New South Wales 2066, Australia.

© Lionel Leventhal Limited, 1982, 1983, 1984
Combined edition © Arms and Armour Press Limited, 1986
All rights reserved. No part of this book may be reproduced or transmitted in any form or by any means, electronic or mechanical, including photocopying, recording or any information storage and retrieval system, without permission in writing from the Publisher.

ISBN 0-85368-757-9

Printed and bound in Great Britain by William Clowes, Beccles, Limited.

PART ONE

◀3

1. (Half-title page) With fire suppression bottle suspended at the ready, an HH-43B patrols near Da Nang Air Base in November 1966. (USAF)
2. (Title spread) A VF-96 F-4B Phantom firing underwing rockets at a Viet Cong stronghold in April 1965. (USN)
3. The setting sun is reflected off rice paddies on the Ca Mau peninsula as a USAF A-1E returns from a strike. (USAF)

▲4

4. Visiting C-119s line the ramp at Bangkok, Thailand, during Operation 'Firm Link', February 1956. Thai, Philippine, and US services mounted a show of force which failed to impress Communist leaders in Cambodia, Laos, or Vietnam. (USAF)

▼5

5. F-84Gs of the 49th Fighter-Bomber Wing are made ready for a mission during 'Firm Link'. (USAF)

6. A Thai security policeman guards an F-100D of the 35th TFS during 'Airlink', a 1957 exercise in Bangkok. (USAF)

6▼

7. Thai workers unload supplies from a C-130A at Bangkok during the Laos crisis of 1959. Red tail and wing markings were worn by US transports when flying over arctic, desert, or jungle regions. (USAF)
8. New Zealand was also interested in keeping South-East Asia peaceful. Airmen of 41 Squadron stand by for inspection with one of their Bristol Freighters during a display in Thailand, June 1962. (USAF)
9. Ten years later, a camouflaged RNZAF Bristol delivers military cargo to South Vietnam. (Via Mesko)

▼7

8▲ 9▼

▲10 ▼11

12▲

10. A Royal Australian Air Force Sabre is refuelled as the ground crew and pilot prepare for joint exercises. (USAF)
11. The first 'Ranch Hand' defoliation aircraft arrived in South Vietnam in January 1962. US Defense Department planners, after conferring with President Kennedy, decided that no attempt would be made to disguise the purpose of the aircraft. (USAF)
12. Initial 'Ranch Hand' missions were designed to remove the ground cover used by the Viet Cong and North Vietnamese when ambushing South Vietnamese road and rail transport. Here a C-123 sprays defoliant beside a Vietnamese highway. (USAF)
13. Martin B-57Bs of the 3rd Bomb Wing line a South Vietnamese Air Base in 1965. Red noses, tail letters, and fuselage stripes identified the 13th Tactical Bomb Squadron, while yellow marked the 8th TBS. (USAF)

13▼

▲14

▲15 ▼16

14. As the air war escalated, Tactical Air Command units were transferred from the US to Pacific Air Forces (PACAF) control. This B-66 at Tan Son Nhut, Saigon in 1965 still carries its TAC shield and lightning bolt on the tail. (USAF)
15. A C-118A prepares to transfer casualties from Tan Son Nhut during heavy rains in 1965. (USAF)
16. The camouflage of this RF-101C was the result of a series of experiments conducted on US-based tactical aircraft in 1963 and 1964. By 1965, the Voodoo had also seen many internal modifications to improve photographic capability and combat survivability. (USAF)
17. Two more Tan Son Nhut RF-101Cs display both the standardized TAC camouflage (with small national insignia) and the earlier experimental camouflage, with its oversized US star. (USAF)
18. Napalm canisters beneath the wings of USAF A-1Es during operations in 1964. (USAF)
19. 'Linda', a C-123 from a US Pacific Air Forces (PACAF) troop carrier unit, in 1964. (USAF)

17▲

18▲ 19▼

▲20

21▲

20. Unbuttoned for maintenance, a Vertol CH-21 stands in the sun at Tan Son Nhut in 1964. The aircraft was probably assigned to the 145th Aviation Battalion, which had assumed control of several light helicopter companies during the previous year. The three-toned camouflage is similar to a scheme adopted by the USAF. (USAF)

21. A 1st Air Commando Squadron A-1E prepares for takeoff from Pleiku Air Base in the Vietnamese Central Highlands near Cambodia in 1966. The original Navy light gull grey and white colours are obvious, but the original tail markings have been replaced by USAF-style codes. (USAF)

22. An assortment of camouflaged and aluminium finish 4th TFW F-105Ds on the flight line at Takhli AB, Thailand in December 1965. (USAF)

22▼

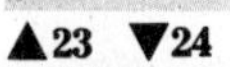

▲23 ▼24

25▲

26▲

23. South Vietnamese A-1Hs in dark brown and green camouflage in 1965. The only national insignia is a small Vietnamese flag on the rudders. (USAF)
24. A 750lb bomb is delivered to an F-100D of the 308th TFS early in 1966. (USAF)
25. South Vietnamese paratroopers tumble from a C-123 during a training exercise in April 1966. (USAF)
26. A Douglas EF-10B of VMCJ-1 landing after a mission to record North Vietnamese radio communications. (USAF)

USAF

WS
0648
MARINES
VE
0472
MARINES

SS.148-2500
SS.152-2500

◀28 29▲

27. (Previous spread) A long exposure captures the motion of maintenance vehicles along the F-100 revetments of the 481st TFS at Tan Son Nhut, July 1968. (USAF)
28. F-4Bs of Marine Fighter-Attack Squadrons 323 and 115 refuelling at the Da Nang hardstand in January 1966. (USAF)
29. Two stars on the door mark this C-47B as the personal aircraft of General Vin Loch, commander of the Vietnamese II Corps. The photograph was taken at the general's headquarters at Pleiku Air Base in 1966. (USAF)
30. T-6 trainers of the Royal Thai Air Force sit on the hardstand at Korat, 1967. (USAF)

30▼

▲31 ▼32

33▲

31. A 429th TFS F-100D *en route* to a Vietnamese target in December 1965. Note the mission symbols on the nose of the aircraft. (USAF)
32. Royal Thai F-86Ls fly formation with a USAF TF-102A during a joint training mission over Thailand in 1966. (USAF)

33. Two 509th Fighter Interceptor Squadron F-102As patrol the skies of South Vietnam in November 1967. (USAF)
34. A black-bellied 8th TFW F-4D has its weapons armed at the 'last chance' checkpoint prior to a September 1972 mission. Alongside is a Royal Thai Air Force T-28. (USAF)

34▼

▲35

35. Its wing set at a high angle of attack, a US Marine Corps F-8E takes off from Da Nang. All-weather Fighter Squadron 235, April 1966. (USAF)

36. Ordnance crews remove 20mm ammunition from the wings of a Navy A-1H after a wheels-up landing at Da Nang in December 1965. (USAF)

37. With external fuel tanks and an ALQ-99 electronic countermeasures pod beneath its wings, a Marine EA-6A prepares for take-off at Da Nang in June 1970. The eagle and lightning bolt insignia belongs to the 1st Composite Reconnaissance Squadron (VMCJ-1). (USAF)

38. Revetted at Da Nang in late 1966, these F-4Cs show their hastily applied camouflage. The original white bellies with large insignia have not been repainted in light grey, and chipped upper-surface paint shows the original light gull grey. (USAF)

39. An airman of the 355th TFW retouches the paint on one of his unit's Republic F-105Ds at Takhli AB, Thailand, 1966. (USAF)

▼36

37▲

38▲ 39▼

▲40 ▼41

42▲

40. A member of the 56th Combat Support Group sprays paint on an HH-3E of Detachment 1, 40th Aerospace Rescue & Recovery Squadron (ARRS) at Nakhon Phanom AB (known as 'NKP' or 'Naked Fanny' by US crews), Thailand, February 1969. (USAF)
41. Men of the 30th ARRS work on the jet engine and transmission of an HH-3C Jolly Green Giant, Udorn AB, Thailand, 1966. (USAF)

42. A Sikorsky HH-3E from Detachment 1, 40th ARRS, stands on the flightline at Nakhon Phanom AB, Thailand in early 1969. The symbols indicating successful missions are stencilled on the fuselage behind the pilot's seat. (USAF)
43. Seen from the open cargo ramp of an HC-130, an HH-53C takes on fuel. Note the pintle-mounted mini-gun in the 'Dutch door' behind the helicopter's pilot. (USAF)

43▼

▲44

44. A camouflaged A-1E sweeps over the Vietnamese jungle during a rescue mission. By 1967, Skyraiders claimed the highest overall loss rate of any aircraft in the theatre – as high as 6.2 per thousand sorties over North Vietnam. (USAF)

45. HC-130s served for command, control, and communications (C^3 or 'Cee-cubed') during rescue missions, with some models providing air-to-air refuelling for HH-3s and HH-53s. HC-130Ps, as seen here, were converted from HC-130Hs and retained the earlier aircraft's Fulton aerial recovery equipment on the nose. The Fulton equipment was never successfully used in South-East Asia. (USAF)

46. Camouflaged to effect, an HC-130P refuels an HH-53C over the Vietnamese countryside. Note the mismatched engine nacelles. (USAF)

47. Only a few USAF HU-16 Albatrosses received this dark blue/white camouflage scheme. Note the wide overspray between the colours. Da Nang, April 1966. (USAF)

▼45

46▲ 47▼

▲48 ▼49

48. Gloss black O-2As, which flew night air-control missions along the Ho Chi Minh Trail, wait on the Nakhon Phanom ramp, 1970. (USAF)

49. The sinister-looking canisters being fitted to the racks of this A-1E carry Spikebuoy sensors to be dropped and planted along the Ho Chi Minh Trail. As part of Project 'Igloo White', the Spikebuoys automatically radioed signals triggered by the vibrations of passing traffic. Nakhon Phanom AB, Thailand, June 1968. (USAF)

50. Flames at the Ubon runway mark the site of the first AC-130A combat loss. Hit by 37mm ground fire over Laos, the gunship returned home with one man dead; a second crewman was killed in the crash, 24 May 1969. (USAF)

50▼

▲51 ▼52

51. An overhauled T56-A turboprop is mounted on an AC-130A of the 16th SOS at Ubon AB, Thailand. The unmatched cowling panels are unlikely to be repainted before operations resume. (USAF)
52. An AC-130A's turboprop engine is removed at a Ubon revetment, June 1969. (USAF)
53. Pave Aegis was the ultimate weapons modification to the AC-130E Spectre gunship – the aftmost 40mm gun was replaced by an Army 105mm howitzer! The throw weight of each round went from 0.6lb to 5.6lb, greatly increasing the chance of destroying a given target while keeping the gunship at a high, safer altitude. (USAF)
54. In position aboard the gunship, final adjustments are made to the howitzer. Flare launchers can be seen in the right foreground. (USAF)
55. An airborne battlefield command and control centre (ABCCC) is inserted into the cargo area of a C-130 at Udorn in late 1971. The pod can be switched to another C-130 during normal aircraft maintenance periods. (USAF)

53▲

54▲ 55▼

▲56 ▼57

58▲

59▲

60▲

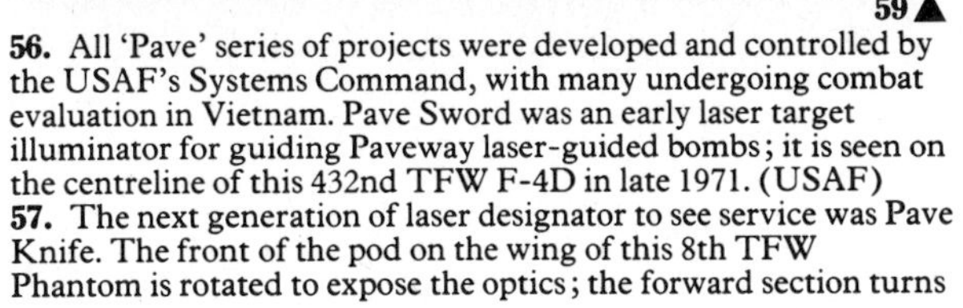

56. All 'Pave' series of projects were developed and controlled by the USAF's Systems Command, with many undergoing combat evaluation in Vietnam. Pave Sword was an early laser target illuminator for guiding Paveway laser-guided bombs; it is seen on the centreline of this 432nd TFW F-4D in late 1971. (USAF)
57. The next generation of laser designator to see service was Pave Knife. The front of the pod on the wing of this 8th TFW Phantom is rotated to expose the optics; the forward section turns upward to protect the lens from dust or gravel. Ubon AB, 1973. (USAF)
58. The smaller, lighter Pave Spike pod could be mounted in a forward Sparrow bay of a Phantom. Pave Spike has remained in service into the 1980s. (USAF)
59. Exposed optics for Pave Spike. 1973. (USAF)
60. Close-up of the Paveway sight mounted in the rear cockpit of an F-4. (USAF)

▲61

61. A US Navy UH-1E lands beside an Army UH-1B on USS *Harnett County* (LST-821) between combat operations in the Mekong Delta. Co Chien River, October 1967. (USN)
62. 1st Air Cavalry troopers arrive by C-130A at Bu Dup Special Forces Camp, during the Cambodian Offensive, May 1970. (USAF)
63. Following a saturation bombing by B-52s in 1966, US Army troopers begin a search and destroy mission as their UH-1D prepares to leave. (USAF)

62▲ 63▼

▲64

▲65 ▼66

64. A Vietnamese Air Force A-1E flies over a 'hootch line' and fortified hamlet in 1964. The US Navy serial number remains on the tail, though the aircraft is painted in an overall grey scheme used by the USAF. (USAF)
65. Maintenance on a turboprop engine of an OV-10 Forward Air Control (FAC) aircraft, Da Nang, September 1970. (USAF)
66. Carrying four marker rockets, a Vietnamese O-1 FAC flies to its patrol area. (USAF)
67. Safety-pins are removed from the bombs and rockets on a pair of VNAF A-37s, Da Nang, September 1970. (USAF)
68. High above South Vietnam, a Canberra of 2 Squadron, RAAF, heads for a strike in March 1970. The Australian unit was based at Phan Rang AB, South Vietnam. (USAF)
69. A handsomely marked A-37 rests in its Vietnamese revetment, September 1969. (USAF)

67▲

68▲ 69▼

▲70 ▼71

72▲

70. A foam-covered F-4C is raised at Bien Hoa in February 1966. Note how the underwing fuel tanks, which protected the lower fuselage and wings, have ruptured and punctured the outboard wing flaps. (USAF)

71. Loaded with napalm canisters, a VNAF A-1H tucks its landing gear away and leaves Da Nang, October 1966. (USAF)

72. A number of Phantoms had light grey painted over tan areas of their camouflage. Though this 16th TRS RF-4C was photographed at Tan Son Nhut in late 1967, other examples were seen in Germany and the USA. (USAF)

73. An Air Force cameraman adjusts his G-suit before boarding a 388th TFW Phantom at Korat AB, June 1970. (USAF)

73▼

▲74

74. Behind a forward catapult aboard USS *America*, an E-2A airborne warning and control aircraft is prepared for its next mission. Across the flight deck, an armed A-6 also awaits orders. September 1970. (USAF)
75. An F-4J of Fighter Squadron 31 returns to USS *Saratoga* following an August 1972 MiG CAP (combat air patrol). (USAF)
76. Armourers load Pave Pat, a sinister-looking fuel-air explosive, onto the wing rack of a 1st SOS A-1E, September 1968. (USAF)

75▶

76 ▲

▲77

▲78

77. 750lb bombs are attached to the MER (Multiple Ejector Rack) of a 428th TFS F-111A before one of the first 'Combat Lancer' missions in March 1968. (USAF)

78. Prior to 'Combat Lancer' (the first deployment of F-111As to South-East Asia) red, white, and blue stripes are painted on the nose of the Detachment Commander's aircraft. 428th TFS, March 1968. (USAF)

79. F-111As returned to combat in September 1972, but encountered a number of critical parts shortages and maintenance problems; seven of fifty-two aircraft were lost. Nevertheless, the 429th TFS (shown) and the 430th TFS flew more than 3,000 missions prior to the signing of the Paris Peace Accords in 1973. (USAF)

80. An F-111A of the 430th TFS out of Takhli, photographed during the unit's last combat mission on 15 August 1973. (USAF)

79▲ 80▼

81. A USAF sergeant checks the 20mm Vulcan gun of a Thailand-based F-105D. A red star stencilled below the cockpit credits the aircraft with one North Vietnamese MiG destroyed. (USAF)
82. An A-1H of Attack Squadron 115 returns to USS *Kitty Hawk* after a strike against the Viet Cong in 1966. (USAF)
83. An A-1E tests the BAK-12 arresting gear at Nakhon Phanom, Thailand in October 1970. Note the black-bellied H-3 and C-123 in the background. (USAF)
84. When the Air National Guard's 188th TFS was activated and ordered to South Vietnam, it came under control of the 31st TFW. One of the squadron's F-100Cs banks over Tuy Hoa before landing. (USAF)
85. High over South Vietnam, an F-100D of the 306th TFS carries two 500lb high drag bombs (outboard racks), two fuel tanks (centre racks), and a pair of napalm bombs (inboard racks). (USAF)

82▶

83▲

84▲ 85▼

▲86 ▼87

86. Maintenance crews install a J-71 engine on an EB-66 of the 41st Tactical Electronic Warfare Squadron (TEWS) at Takhli, Thailand, September 1969. (USAF)
87. A 42nd TEWS (attached to the 355th TFW) EB-66 approaches a KC-135 for refuelling, March 1970. (USAF)
88. A Strategic Air Command KC-135 climbs out of U-Tapao AB, Thailand, on an aerial refuelling mission, 1970. (USAF)
89. UH-1Ps were flown by the USAF on psychological warfare missions and air base defence activities. 1967. (USAF)
90. MiG combat air patrol. A formation of 33rd TFW F-4Es and 432nd TRW F-4Ds patrol for enemy jets. Missiles, guns, and ECM pods for air-to-air combat can be seen in this 1972 photograph. (USAF)

88▲

89▲ 90▼

91. Hercules transports provided much of Australia's heavy airlift support. (Via Mesko)
92. An SH-3 hovers over the fantail of the US destroyer *Benner* off the coast of Vietnam. (USAF)
93. Although the overall engine grey scheme was a standard for Navy SH-3s, most of the Sea Kings carried high-visibility markings and insignia. The story behind this duller scheme is unknown. (USAF)

91▶

▼92

93▼

▲94

▲95 ▼96

97▲

94. An F-4J of Marine Fighter-Attack Squadron 542 taxis out of Da Nang, May 1966. (USAF)
95. The Republic of Korea sent troops to Vietnam, but left the air war to the USAF and VNAF. Although this red and white Cessna Skymaster was used in support of the Koreans, it is not certain in what role. (Via Mesko)

96. Following a December 1968 mission over South Vietnam, two 557th TFS F-4Cs return to Cam Ranh Bay AB. (USAF)
97. A Grumman S-2C target tug aircraft stands at the catapult prior to launch from USS *Bennington.* (USAF)
98. An RC-135D, used to collect electronic Intelligence data, approaches a KC-135 for refuelling, January 1967. (USAF)

98▼

▲99 ▼100

99. UH-1Bs of the 101st Airborne Division are offloaded from a Military Airlift Command C-133 at Tan Son Nhut Air Base. Elements of the 'Screamin' Eagles' had previously fought in Vietnam, but in late 1967 the entire division arrived during operation 'Eagle Thrust'. (USAF)
100. The long shadows of a late December afternoon wash this Lockheed C-130A near Cam Ranh Bay in 1966. (USAF)
101. A Huey of the US Army's 1st Aviation Brigade lifts off from Tan Son Nhut Air Base in May 1970. The 1st, one of the largest commands in South Vietnam, had been headquartered at Tan Son Nhut before moving to Long Binh in December 1967. (USAF)
102. An Air Force sergeant – wearing 'uniform of the day' for Thailand – paints the canopy rail of a 307th TFS Phantom in the squadron colour. Air and ground crew names would be stencilled on the left and right sides respectively. Udorn AB, October 1972. (USAF)

101▲ 102▼

103. With its US Army markings overpainted, this patchwork C-7A and its US Air Force crew prepare to leave Phu Cat in June 1967. (USAF)
104. The Strategic Air Command's 99th Aerial Refueling Squadron took their 'Ramrod' callsign seriously – it could be found painted on the forward fuselage of most of the unit's KC-135s. (USAF)
105. Troops search for survivors at the crash site of a UH-1D near the Cambodian border in December 1968. (USAF)
106. Pilot and Weapons Systems Operator of a 58th TFS F-4E deplane at Udorn AB, Thailand in late 1972. Spreader bars allow each bomb rack to carry two Sidewinders in addition to the normal three-bomb load. (USAF)

▲103 ▼104

▼105

106▶

▲107

▲108 ▼109

107. 20mm Vulcan gun pods move to Vietnam with the 49th TFW in May 1972 as part of the US response to the North Vietnamese spring offensive. (USAF)
108. Members of the 49th TFW prepare their F-4Ds for deployment to South-East Asia in May 1972. (USAF)
109. Refuelling high over Thailand, an A-7D of the 354th TFW engages the boom of a KC-135 tanker. Coloured segments of the boom help the boom operator (known as the 'boomer' or 'gas-passer') to gauge the distance between the two aircraft. (USAF)
110. Engine start at dusk for an A-26K at Nakhon Phanom. The bottom of the aircraft, as well as its load of napalm bombs, has been painted black for night operations. (USAF)
111. Bombs are loaded aboard a B-52D at U-Tapao AB, Thailand, in September 1972. (USAF)
112. (Overleaf)A-7Ds of the 354th TFW disappear against the camouflaged hardstand at Korat AB, Thailand, October 1972. (USAF)

110▲ 111▼

MB
MB
MB
MB

▲113

▲114

113. An F-4E of the 421st TFS prepares for its final bombing mission of the Vietnam War, 15 August 1973. (USAF)
114. A sharkmouthed 388th TFW F-105 is prepared for the trip home as the wing redeploys from Thailand to the USA in August 1973. (USAF)
115. Credited with three MiG kills as an F-105F, this aircraft was modified to an F-105G for 'Wild Weasel' anti-SAM missions with the 561st TFS. Photographed at Korat AB, Thailand before returning to the USA in August 1973, the same aircraft is now part of the US Air Force Museum collection at Wright-Patterson AFB, Ohio. (USAF)
116. An A-26K of the 609th Special Operations Squadron sweeps over flooded plains near Nakhon Phanom AB, Thailand July 1969. (USAF)

115▲ 116▼

▲117

▲118

▲119 ▼120

117. The President of the Philippines arrives at Clark Air Base in his Fokker F-27 to greet repatriated US POWs. The Americans were interviewed and given medical examinations at the US base in the Philippines prior to being shipped home. (USAF)

118. 'Enhance Plus' was an accelerated re-supply effort to help South Vietnamese forces fill the vacuum left by the withdrawing Americans. A VNAF C-123K taxis past C-130As at Tan Son Nhut following a hasty transfer. November 1972. (USAF)

119. Additional reconnaissance was provided by AQM-34 drones, which were launched and controlled by DC-130 Hercules aircraft. Udorn, 8 April 1975. (USAF)

120. April 1975 was the last month of two separate Vietnams. As the final North Vietnamese campaign began, this U-2R reconnaissance plane was photographed at U-Tapao AB, Thailand. The yellow stand in the foreground gives access to the cockpit while providing shade from the sun. (USAF)

PART TWO

1. A Boeing Vertol CH-46 of HMM-265 accelerates out of the landing zone as part of a multi-battalion Marine Corps force moves off in search of the enemy, Quang Nam, 1966. (USMC)

169
MARINES
EP
52504

2. Callsign 'Hobo', a Douglas A-1E Skyraider of the 1st SOS, taxies at Ubon RTAFB to cover a December 1968 rescue mission. The bullet-shaped pods on the outboard wing racks are LAU-3 rocket launchers; inboard are two bomblet dispensers, and closest to the landing gear is a mini-gun pod; the same stores are mounted beneath the left wing. (Piccirillo)

3. 'Jungle Jim' was the first unit of the new US Air Commandos, and 'Farm Gate' was their first deployment to South Vietnam. In 1961 they were equipped with North American T-28 trainers and Douglas B-26 bombers. The following year they became involved in combat operations. This T-28D Trojan, armed with bombs and rockets, is seen over South Vietnam in 1962. (USAF)

4. Col. Nguyen Cao Ky, commander of the Vietnamese Air Force, inspects the 514th Fighter Squadron, VNAF, in December 1963. Eighteen months later, Ky would be appointed Premier of the Republic of Vietnam. (USAF)

▲3 ▼4

5▲

6▲

5. When the Vietnamese Air Force requested replacements for its Grumman F8F Bearcats in 1959, the American Military Assistance Advisory Group (MAAG) considered obsolete Navy AD-4 Skyraiders. Procurement and refitting difficulties led to the assignment of AD-6s, which were then still operational with Navy air groups. Six were sent in September 1960, and 25 more in May 1961. In 1962 the AD-6 was redesignated A-1H. (USAF)

6. In the days before camouflage, VNAF A-1s displayed flashy fuselage unit identification bands. These A-1H Skyraider fighter-bombers, seen at Bien Hoa Air Base in September 1962, are in USAF grey overall; although similar, the US Navy scheme used a different grey with white belly and control surfaces. (USAF)

▼7 ▲8

7. Armed T-28 trainers were delivered to the Vietnamese in 1959, despite VNAF hopes for jets, as flown by the Thais, Filipinos, and Nationalist Chinese. Even had Vietnamese maintenance facilities been capable of handling more sophisticated equipment, the Geneva Agreements of July 1954 had banned the introduction of jet aircraft to Vietnam. These well-armed North American T-28Bs stand alert at Bien Hoa in 1962. (USAF)

8. Led by their American instructor, Vietnamese paratroops clip their static lines and await the green light to jump. The overhead wire was designed at a comfortable height for the average American paratrooper, and required a longer reach for most Vietnamese. (USAF)

9. Vietnamese paratroopers jump from USAF C-123 Providers during an airshow near Saigon in December 1964. Parachute assaults proved impracticable over most of Vietnam and were superceded by helicopter assaults, which could land and extract a fighting force with more control. (USAF)

9▲

▲10

▲11 ▼12

10. A line-up of Vietnamese Army Cessna O-1F Birddog forward air control aircraft photographed at Bien Hoa in January 1966. The aircraft were painted a glossy forest green overall. (USAF)

11. A drone launch at Ky Hoa Island. These Marines are launching MQM-39 drones as targets for Hawk surface-to-air missile batteries, December 1965. Although US anti-aircraft missiles were deployed and tested throughout the war, their use was never required. (USN)

12. The primary Marine Corps helicopter of the early war years was the Sikorsky H-34 Choctaw. Here an H-34 of Marine Airlift Group 36 crosses a beach during amphibious operations north of Chu Lai in November 1965. (USAC)

13. Cartridge starter smoke blows from a North American F-100D Supersabre of the 481st Tactical Fighter Squadron in the revetment area of Tan Son Nhut, 1965. Although hardened structures on three sides provided protection from exploding neighbouring aircraft, forward-firing munitions could easily strike aircraft in facing revetments! (USAF)

14. Refuelling F-100Ds at Bien Hoa in early 1966. A massive building programme during the latter half of 1965 had produced enough revetments to shelter most of Bien Hoa's aircraft, but refuelling operations still took place on open hardstands. Such groups of exposed aircraft were rarely singled out for Communist mortar or rocket attacks. (USAF)

13▲ 14▼

15. The Vietcong lobbed sixteen rounds into Binh Thuy Air Base during the early hours of 11 September 1968, but with little effect. They returned that evening with forty more rounds, damaging 21 aircraft and destroying two. The remains of this VNAF H-34 illustrate the protective capabilities of an engine firewall, though in theory the rest of the aircraft was meant to have been saved! (USAF)

16. Although used extensively during early US involvement in the war, the Piasecki Vertol H-21 simply was not adeqate for helicopter assaults. The small exits were too high to allow the rapid deployment of troops, whose movement was further restricted by the presence of door gunners. (USAF)

15▲ 16▼

17▲ 18▼

17. The only Vietcong attack on Bien Hoa in 1965 saw almost 100 mortars and rockets fired on the night of 23/24 August. Eleven aircraft, including this Bell UH-1 Iroquois, were damaged and 29 servicemen wounded. The attackers retired without loss. (USAF)

18. Terrorist attacks on billets and Saigon hotels resulted in a US Presidential dependent evacuation order in early 1965. The families of servicemen and contractors were flown out by both military and civil transports. (USAF)

24231
U.S. AIR FORCE
FH-231
24328
U.S. AIR FORCE
FH-328
24284
U.S. AIR FORCE
FH-284

▲19 ▼20

U.S. AIR FORCE
0144

21▲

19. Two of these F-105 Thunderchiefs of 18th Tactical Fighter Wing, en route to targets in North Vietnam in 1965, carry AGM-12 Bullpup missiles beneath their wings and drop tanks mounted on the centreline; the other Thunderchief is armed with conventional bombs and has two wing-mounted drop tanks. Inefficient visual sighting of the radio-guided Bullpups, combined with their small payload, paved the way for laser-guided and electro-optically guided bombs weighing in excess of 2,000lb. (USAF)
20. The Boeing B-52F Stratofortress served over Vietnam between June 1965 and April 1966, at which time the variant was replaced by the D-model. The B-52F illustrated, 57-0144, was later named 'Mekong Express' and flew 86 missions before rotating home. Gloss black under surfaces with silver sides and tops were peculiar to the F-model. (USAF)
21. The question of the Boeing B-47 Stratojet's suitability for conventional bombing over Vietnam was obviated by the lack of younger aircrews with flying hours logged in the type. A squadron manned by older, full colonels and brigadier generals would have robbed many other units of their experienced leadership! A few EB-47s did serve in Vietnam, gathering electronic intelligence. This photograph was taken at Tan Son Nhut on 13 April 1966, shortly after a mortar attack. (USAF)

22. Little has been published about the US Navy's flying-boats in Vietnam, or their coastal patrols. Here, the door gunner of a Martin P-5 Marlin breakfasts at his station during a long mission. (USN)

23. A Douglas A-1H Skyraider of Navy Attack Squadron 52 cruises over 10/10 cloud covering the Gulf of Tonkin in November 1966. The Navy used the Skyraider until April 1968, when it was retired as the last prop-driven attack aircraft in their inventory. (USAF)

24. Some of the Navy's McDonnell Douglas EA-3B Skywarriors wore incredible camouflages of greys and blues. 'Gear down and dirty', speed brakes deployed, this Skywarrior approaches NAS Agana, Guam, in September 1972. (Bishop)

25. An A-1E of the 1st Air Commando Squadron, 1966. (USAF)

▲**22** ▼**23**

24▲ 25▼

▲26 ▼27

26. Air Force FACs inherited hundreds of Cessna 0-1s when the Army lost command of its own fixed-wing observation fleet. This Birddog was photographed at Bien Hoa in July 1965 with its forward half in Air Force colours and its tail in an unusual Army scheme. (Menard)
27. Students of camouflage are hard-pressed to explain the light blue and grey scheme applied to this Cessna A-37. The aircraft is seen on a mission in August 1967. (USAF)
28. Its wing racks empty, an Air Force A-1E Skyraider rolls through the clouds near the Saigon River to strafe a Vietcong target, 1966. Smoke from earlier passes can be seen at the lower left corner of the photograph. (USAF)
29. The 'One-oh-wonderful' McDonnell RF-101 Voodoo reconnaissance aircraft had a greater dash speed and carried larger cameras than the McDonnell Douglas RF-4 Phantom II that eventually replaced it. This photograph of a Voodoo taxiing back at Tan Son Nhut in 1965 shows one of several two-tone green camouflages worn by RF-101s in South-East Asia. (USAF)

28▲ 29▼

USAF
USAF

◀30 31▲

30. 750lb bombs drop from four F-105 Thunderchiefs on a mission in June 1966. The two 'Thuds' at the left of the formation are painted in the standard camouflage pattern; the one on the right wears a reversed image, and the McDonnell Douglas EB-66 Destroyer and the fourth 105 are unpainted. (USAF)

31. Nationalist Chinese civilian contractors apply a coat of camouflage paint to a Thunderchief at a depot in Taiwan in 1966. The rush to camouflage tactical aircraft produced many unusual colours and patterns, though the standard scheme is being applied here. (USAF)

32. The USAF's initial F-4C Phantoms wore the Navy paint scheme of grey with white undersides and control surfaces. When tactical camouflage was introduced in 1966, upper surfaces were to be painted a pattern of two greens and a tan with light grey below. The Phantom on the right is still in Navy colours, while the one on the left has the new upper surface camouflage, but still retains the Navy white belly. (USAF)

32▼

▲33 ▼34

33. The camouflage paint of this F-4C Phantom seems much the worse for wear in this early 1967 photograph. The tips of the wing tanks and the top of the vertical tail are yellow, a squadron colour, but further identification is difficult in this pre-unit code era. (USAF)

34. Most of the war's heavy bombing missions were flown by Boeing B-52Ds, which wore three-tone green camouflage on top with gloss black on the bottom and sides. A cell of three 'Buffs' (Big, ugly, fat fellows) at altitude could string a corridor of 324 bombs across a target. Vietcong prisoners complained that they rarely knew an attack was in progress until the bombs began exploding around them. (USAF)

▲35 ▼36

37▲ 38▼

39▼

35. Marines board a CH-46 Sea Knight helicopter during operations from the amphibious assault ship USS *Princeton* in April 1967. Laid down as an Essex class aircraft carrier during the Second World War, *Princeton* had been converted for Marine helicopter operations in 1959. Note the over-painted white areas in the fuselage star insignias. (USN)
36. A pair of Marine Sikorsky H-34s over artillery positions in the Mekong Delta region, early 1967. (USN)
37. Most of Nha Trang Air Base was closed by flooding during the rains of January 1966, providing this aircrewman with an opportunity to cast his fishing line. Even when the foot-deep waters receded, the base was thick with mud for weeks. (USAF)
38. Armament crews continue to load their A-1 Skyraiders in a downpour, as the clouds clear over the mountains in the background. (USAF)
39. Weather was a factor in the operations of both sides, especially during the monsoon season. This composite photograph, taken by the Essa IV weather satellite in June 1967, shows heavy cloud cover over the border between the two Vietnams and Laos and Cambodia. Typhoon 'Anita' boils in the South China Sea at the upper right of the photograph. (USAF)

▲40

40, 41. A Royal Thai Air Transport Command Avro (Hawker Siddeley) 748 photographed at Ubon in October 1968. The blue trim and orange fin and wing-tips are common to both sides of the aircraft, but the legend on the portside is in English while that on the starboard is in Thai. (Piccirillo)

42. A rare view of a Laotian Douglas C-47 Skytrain visiting Ubon in March 1969. (Piccirillo)

43. A formation of Australian Sabre Mk. 32s flown by No. 79 Squadron, RAAF. Based at Ubon, Thailand, the Sabres were photographed from a USAF Phantom in 1968. (Piccirillo)

▼41

42▲ 43▼

▲44

▲45

▲46 ▼47

48▲

49▲

44–47. A dramatic sequence showing an A-1H 'Sandy' (Skyraider) of the 602nd SOS (Special Operations Squadron) making an emergency landing at NKP in December 1968. While covering a search and rescue mission near Tchepone, Laos, a 37mm hit in the left wing root destroyed the hydraulic system, necessitating a wheels-up, flaps-up landing. **44.** The approach with arresting hook down. **45.** Easing closer to the runway, the canopy already jettisonned. **46.** Impact on the foamed runway.
47. Rescue crews secure the aircraft while a fire tender and Kaman HH-43 'Pedro' stand by. (Piccirillo)
48. 'OK, the excitement's over!' Firemen 'slosh' through foam after extinguishing a fire on a battle-damaged Douglas AC-47, whose left engine had been hit by enemy ground fire, 1969. (USAF)
49. A giant salvage crane, nicknamed 'Big Tilly', raises a damaged McDonnell Douglas Phantom II of 559th Tactical Fighter Squadron at Cam Rahn Bay Air Base in 1967. (USAF)

▲50 ▼51

52▲ 53▼

50. This Air Force Cessna 0-1E Birddog melts into its background, the defence works of a Vietnamese hamlet. The upper wing panels were later painted orange or white to emphasize the slow-moving Forward Air Controller's (FAC) position to friendly strike aircraft. (USAF)
51. Low, slow, and vulnerable: a Cessna 0-1 and an 0-2 (left) launch marker rockets near Phan Rang in July 1969. Rockets were rarely expected to hit their targets, instead the strike aircraft were directed to aim a certain range and azimuth from the marker. (USAF)
52. 'Little Tuff', a Cessna 0-1G of the 19th Tactical Air Support Squadron at Bien Hoa in 1967. White phosphorus marker rockets are mounted beneath the wings. (USAF via Bishop)
53. An unusual dog's jaw and tongue insignia painted on a USAF Birddog FAC. An American pilot and Vietnamese observer plan their mission together. (USAF)

▲54 ▼55

54. Four of the 315th Strategic Operations Wing's Provider squadrons were engaged in assault airlift operations, delivering supplies and personnel to forward combat locations. This Fairchild C-123K of 19th Special Operations Squadron shows the white wing-tip and tail markings used to warn off friendly support aircraft during low-level flights and combat zone landings. The main and nose gear doors have been removed to improve rough strip landing and take-off characteristics. (USAF)

55. Leaflets fly from a Douglas C-47 Skytrain along the South Vietnamese coast. During January 1966 alone, safe conduct leaflets were used as passes by over 1,600 defecting Vietcong. (USAF)

56, 57. The 5th Special Operations Squadron's U-10B Courier psychological warfare operations were generally limited to leaflet drops and recording broadcasts. The top photograph (**56**) was taken in 1966, shortly after the unit had dropped its one hundred millionth leaflet and broadcast its one-thousandth hour of tape. Note the removed gear strut fairings and the unusual presentation of the entire serial number (63-13111) on the tail. **57** is a 1968 shot from the same unit, with the wing painted high visibility white. The serial 66-14374 reduces to 66-374 below the squadron code letters. Leaflets cover the tail wheel and strut, held in place by the slipstream. (USAF)

56▲ 57▼

▲58

58. In its last year of operations, the 9th Special Operations Squadron added to its inventory Cessna 0-2B Super Skymasters, which carried loudspeakers on the rear fuselage. The squadron was inactivated at Tan Son Nhut on 29 February 1972. (USAF)

59. The North American (Rockwell) OV-10 Bronco was designed as the Counter Insurgency (COIN) aircraft of the mid-1960s, at a time when jets were not planned for brushfire wars such as Vietnam. With the Tonkin Gulf Resolution, the US no longer voluntarily withheld its jets, and the OV-10 went into combat as the most powerful of the light FACs. The Bronco was often as capable of destroying a target as marking it. (USAF)

60. A Bell UH-1 at Tuy Hoa. (Cross)

61. Aircrews rarely flew the same aircraft on each mission. Kill markings were painted to represent the total score of the aircraft rather than any individual. McDonnell Douglas F-4D Phantom No. 463 downed her sixth enemy aircraft on 15 October 1972 when Majors McCoy and Brown nailed a MiG-21. More famous was the aircraft's fifth victory on 28 August 1972 which, coincidentally, was the fifth for Captain Steve Ritchie, making him the first American ace of the war. That victory was the fourth for back-seater Captain Charles De Bellevue, who would eventually score two more kills to become America's top MiG killer of the war. (USAF)

▼59

60▲ 61▼

62▲ 63▼

64▲ 65▼

62. A-1H Skyraiders with USAF camouflage show their Vietnamese Air Force insignia. (USAF)
63. Early Navy operations in Vietnam included combat training with Lockheed DP-2E Neptunes and BQM-34 target drones. The colourful aircraft seen here belonged to VC-5 at Da Nang in December 1965. (USN)
64. The 'Ranch Hand' defoliation headquarters was at Nha Trang. 'Agent Orange' spray missions could be flown by USAF or VNAF crews with aircraft from a common pool. At the time of this early 1969 photograph, an American star insignia had been slipped into the fuselage brackets of this Fairchild C-123K Provider. (USAF)
65. Three 'Ranch Hand' C-123 Providers in 1966, at the onset of tactical camouflage paint. On the day this photograph was taken, the trio was flown by VNAF crews, and the aircraft wore temporary VNAF fuselage insignia. To facilitate retransfer to the USAF, the Vietnamese fin flash is not applied, nor are any wing insignia carried. (USAF)

▲66

66. One of the first gunships delivered to Vietnam was this Douglas AC-47, photographed at Bien Hoa in 1965. Single-barrelled 30-calibre machine-guns fired through four positions in the rear door, two in the open doorway, and two more in the windows aft of the wing. The artwork on the nose of the aircraft shows the cartoon character 'Snuffy Smith' quoting cowboy star Roy Rodgers' 'Git 'em, Bullit!' (USAF, via Bishop)

67. The AC-47's firepower was increased by changing the weapons from single-barrelled 30-calibres to three rotary-barrelled 7.62mm miniguns. Note the yellow mission marks stencilled on the wing root beneath the centre gun. (USAF)

68. A time exposure showing an AC-47's tracers at work. Flying in a counter-clockwise circle, the pilot would drop his left wing and sight over his left shoulder, concentrating his fire at the apex of a deadly cone. (USAF)

69, 70. Fairchild AC-119Gs (codenamed 'Shadow'), the armed version of the C-119 Flying Boxcars, were flown by the 17th Special Operations Squadron, while Fairchild AC-119Ks ('Stinger') came under the 18th SOS. These photographs show (**69**) US and Vietnamese crew in front of a second 17th SOS aircraft (tail number 0-25942), and (**70**) a 'Shadow' flight in daylight in 1971. (USAF)

▼67

68▲

69▲ 70▼

▲71 ▼72

71. An unarmed Fairchild AC-119 arrives at Nha Trang in December 1968, a special Christmas arrival for the 71st Special Operations Squadron. (USAF via Bishop)

72. 'Candlestick' was a Fairchild C-123 Provider flareship operation of the 606th SOS at Nakhon Phanom AB, Thailand. Vietcong and North Vietmanese night assaults and infiltrations brought American night interdiction aircraft into roles that had not been envisaged by Defense Department planners. (Piccirillo)

73. A spin-off of the C-123 Provider flareship saw high intensity lights mounted beneath C-123s and Lockheed C-130s. A two-mile radius was bathed in constant light with the aircraft at an altitude of 12,000ft. Although the lights had far longer duration than flares, their fixed position on the aircraft increased the danger from ground fire. (USAF)

74. One of the lesser known modifications of the war was 'Black Spot', the Fairchild NC-123K night interdiction aircraft. Special night optics helped find the enemy, while bomblet dispensers in the belly helped destroy him. The camouflage colours shown here are two greens and black on top and two greys underneath. (Piccirillo)

73▲ 74▼

▲75 ▼76

75, 76. One of the Lockheed P-2H Neptunes used by the Army to gather electronic intelligence (ELINT). Still wearing Navy colours – grey with a white top – the aircraft were attached to the 1st Radio Research Company. **76** shows the 1st Radio Research Co.'s emblem on the nose of a second P-2: a 'crazy cat' with double-barbed lance riding a winged horse. (Piccirillo)
77. A surprising number of support aircraft became essential to American combat missions. The C-7 radio relay ship aided in command and control of different elements of an attack force. (USAF)
78. 'Combat Lightning' was the codename of seven Boeing KC-135As used by SAC (Strategic Air Command) for communications relay. Note the dorsal antennas, a distinguishing feature of this variant. The engine covers have been removed for maintenance. (USAF)
79. Modified with special low-light level TV cameras, the Martin B-57G Night Intruder was one of the more effective night attack aircraft flying against the Ho Chi Minh Trail. 'FK' was the trail code of the 13th Tactical Bomb Squadron, one of the oldest attack units in the USAF. (USAF)

77▲

78▲ 79▼

80. Marine EF-10Bs of VMCJ-1 operated on electronic countermeasure missions using the most advanced electronics of the day. Somewhat of an anachronism, the Korean War vintage Skyknights had never been fitted with ejection seats! (Piccirillo)
81. McDonnell Douglas EB-66 Destroyers from the 42nd Tactical Electronic Warfare Squadron were used to jam SAM acquisition radars and fighter ground control interception systems. These converted bombers often orbited beyond the approach and exit corridors planned for a high threat target, masking the attack force. (USAF)

80▼ 81▲

▲82 ▼83

82. Although its own early-warning radars were limited by ground effect, the Lockheed EC-121 Warning Star assembled information from all sources in their capacity as airborne command post for all missions flown north of the twentieth parallel. The codename was 'College Eye', 1967. (USAF)
83. EC-121Rs, though not mounting the airborne radar of their cousins, also served as 'College Eye' mission control aircraft during missions in the North. This photograph shows a 'College Eye' orbit over the Gulf of Tonkin, a safe distance from anti-aircraft weapons. (USAF)
84. Air Delivered Seismic Intruder Devices (ADSIDs) are loaded beneath the wing of a Navy Lockheed SP-2H in 1968. Dropped along suspected infiltration routes, the ADSIDs transmitted electronic signals from vibrations of passing traffic. By assembling data from several such sources, the 'Igloo White' project could direct air strikes or ground missions to where they would be most effective.
85. Regular North Vietnamese Army operations made some use of radio for control and communications. The job of Douglas EC-47s, such as this example from the 360th TEWS (1970), was to intercept and record those signals. (USAF)

84▲ 85▼

86. Guided by a McDonnell Douglas EB-66 Destroyer, which also jammed enemy defences before fighters began carrying their own ECM pods, a flight of newly camouflaged F-4C Phantoms drops its bombs over North Vietnam. The attacks during July 1966 began the assault on North Vietnamese oil storage facilities. (USAF)

87. 'Wild Weasel' missile suppression sweeps became part of the regular escort 'up North' as defences became more sophisticated. This F-105F Thunderchief unloads its six centreline 500-pounders over a surface-to-air missile (SAM) site, 1967. An AGM-45 Shrike missile is mounted on the outboard wing station. (USAF)

◀86 87▼

▲88 ▼89

88. Lyndon Johnson once hoped that his Presidency would never have to be remembered for its foreign policies, but fate dealt him the Vietnam problem. The President visited south-east Asia in December 1967, where he is seen disembarking from aircraft 26000, better known as 'Air Force One'. (USAF)

89. A full load of 2.75in rockets wobbles crazily after launch from an F-100D during a close air support mission in 1967. The Supersabre was known as the 'Hun' to its crews, a name derived from the hundred of its designation. (USAF)

90. Electronic jamming diverts a SAM into the ground, as bombs explode on Phuc Yen Airfield, North Vietnam. A Navy aircraft took this unusual photograph during a joint mission against the MiG base in October 1967. (USN)

91. Tactical airlift often included some rough landings, such as this one endured by a Fairchild C-123 bringing supplies to an unimproved strip in 1966. (USAF)

92. Camouflaged Lockheed F-104C Starfighters of the 435th Tactical Fighter Squadron seen from a tanker in October 1966. Slippages in McDonnell Douglas F-4D production delayed retirement of the 104 by five years, the last of the Starfighters leaving Thailand in 1967. (USAF)

90▲

91▲ 92▼

▲93

93. A Grumman A-6A Intruder of VA-35 ('The Panthers') banks over the Gulf of Tonkin in June 1968. Twenty-four high-drag 500-pounders are divided among four wing racks, while a fifth multiple ejector rack (MER) is empty on the centreline. (USN)
94. Swing-wing General Dynamics F-111As of the 428th TFS arrived in Thailand in March 1968 and began operations almost immediately. The loss of three aircraft halted operations in late April, and the detachment returned to the US in November after only a few more missions. Returning with enhanced F-111As in 1972, the 429th and 430th TFSs redeemed the aircraft's reputation by flying twenty strikes over North Vietnam without escort or refuelling in monsoon weather that grounded all other aircraft. (USAF)
95. 'Shrapnel Apartments', an Air Force electronics outpost ten miles from North Vietnam. Stations like this were frequent targets for Communist shellings and occasional frontal assaults. (USAF)
96. Napalm bombs fall from an early Cessna A-37A Dragonfly in 1969. Tail fins were removed from the thin shelled bomb casings, producing a tumbling action that spread the destructive effect over a wide area. Though used in the Second World War and the Korean War, napalm became a centre of controversy. (USAF)

▼94

MORTAR
SQUARE
VACANCY
SHRAPNEL APTS
BY BOOM MANAGEMENT
AIR CONDITIONED BY 81 mm MORTARS
HARD WOOD FLOORS
SCREENED IN PATIOS
FALLOUT SHELTERS

95▲ 96▼

USAF

▲97

▲98 ▼99

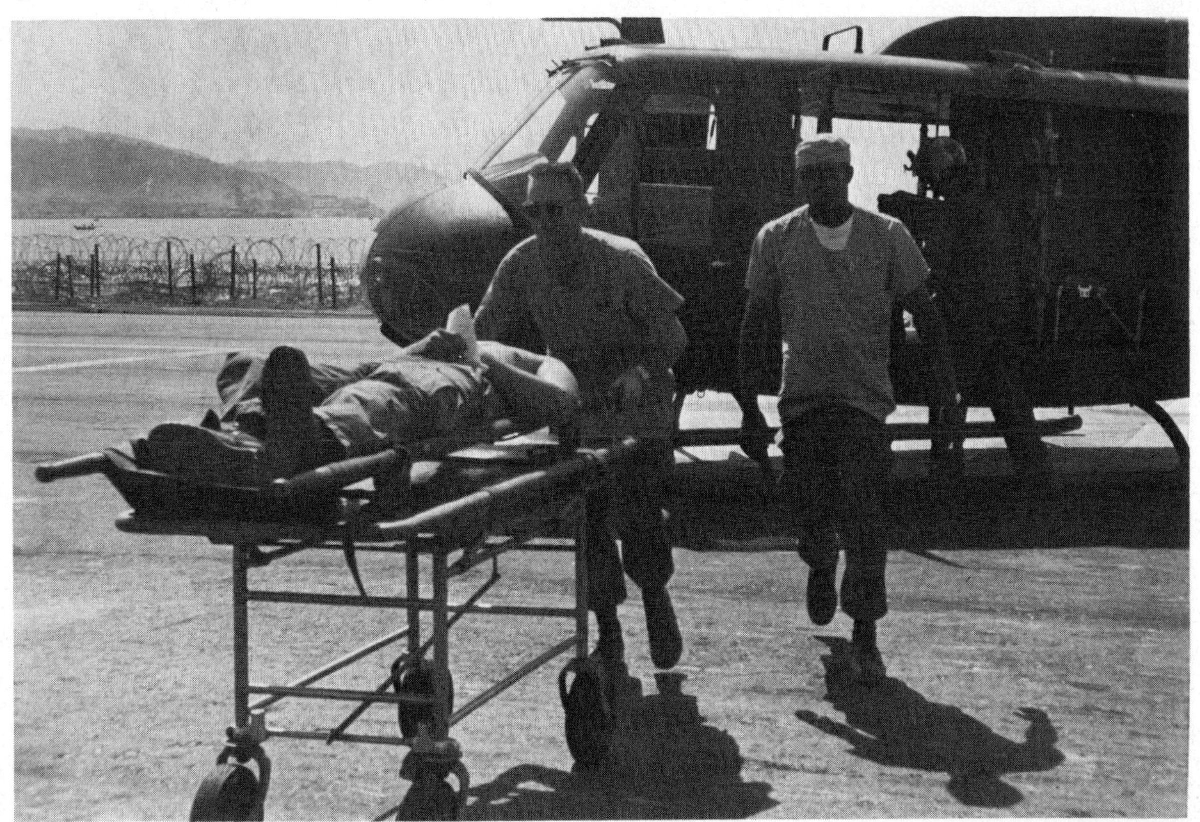

100▲ 101▼

97. The A-37 proved to be a reliable, if somewhat small, tactical support aircraft. The Mk 82 500-pounder released by this 604th SOS 'Tweet' appears quite massive in scale. (USAF)
98. Ordered by the US Army, De Havilland Canada C-7 Caribous were turned over to the USAF when the Army lost command of its own fixed wing tactical airlift. This aircraft was taken over by the 459th TAS. (USAF)
99. An early Sikorsky HH-3E Jolly Green Giant, without the external refuelling boom on the right-hand side of the fuselage. Rescue helicopters made tempting targets for ground gunners, but gun positions behind the cockpit and on the rear ramp helped reduce the temptation. (USAF)
100. Medical air evacuation approached a zenith in Vietnam, where it was reported that a wounded soldier could be in a field hospital quicker than a US car crash victim could be saved. When red cross markings encouraged ground fire, Army UH-1 'dust-off' missions were flown without the markings. (USAF)
101. The Marine Corps, like the Army, found the helicopter gunship concept early in the fighting, and pressed for its development as 'flying artillery'. Here, a Marine UH-1E Huey launches a pair of rockets against Vietcong ridge positions in 1971. (USMC)

▲102

103▶

102. An Air Force Kaman HH-43 lands on the helicopter pad of the hospital ship USS *Repose.* Patients were transferred from the ship to Da Nang, where Military Airlift Command transports evacuated them to the United States. (USAF)

103. The recovery of downed helicopters and aircraft was a priority mission for both the Army and the Marines. Here, an Army CH-47 Chinook transports a Bell UH-1. Removing the tail and main rotors lightened the Huey, which would have been too heavy to transport at combat weight. (Boeing-Vertol via Bishop)

UNITED STATES ARMY

▲104

104. 'Leprechaun', a Bell AH-1 Cobra of the 1st Air Cavalry Division climbs out of a forward refuelling zone. Note the portable pumps and 55-gallon fuel drums in the background, May 1970. (USAF)
105. Downed by gunfire? Not quite; this pair of Army Hueys landed in a stream near the base of An Khe so the crews could wash off the accumulated dust and dirt. (USAF)
106. 'Excedrin Headache No. 10,003' is mounted beneath a Sikorsky CH-54 of the 1st Air Cavalry. A fuse extender exploded the five-ton bomb just above ground level, clearing trees and opening landing zones for following helicopters. Nicknamed 'Big Mother', this Skycrane carries credits for two previous missions, Da Nang, October 1968. (USAF)
107. Plastic water bags, packed in shock resistant canisters, tumble from a Boeing-Vertol CH-46 resupplying a forward Marine company in 1967.

▼105

106▲ 107▼

▲108

▲109

108. Unlike the Second World War, the Vietnam War produced few aces. Mission tallies were more impressive to count; here a pilot of the 558th TFS is presented with a 200 mission ace after a December 1967 sortie. (USAF)
109. 'Chicago 02' gets a second kill. On 5 June 1967, Captains Richard Pascoe and Norman Wells paint a red star on their McDonnell Douglas F-4C after downing a MiG-17 with a Sidewinder. Their previous victory together had been a MiG-21 burned by a Sparrow on 6 January 1967. (USAF)
110. Troops of the 1st Air Cavalry Division drop from a UH-1D Slick ('Slicks' were troop carriers, 'Hogs' were gunships) in April 1967. The Huey was already the standard Army assault helicopter, used in nearly every 'in-country' mission. (US Army)

110▶

▲111

▲112 ▼113

111. A 3rd TFW North American F-100 Supersabre snags the arrestor cable at Bien Hoa after its drag parachute failed to deploy. Ground arresting systems usually took longer to stop an aircraft than did shipboard rigs, since few Air Force aircraft were stressed for short carrier landings. (USAF)
112. Australian 'Cranberry' pilots amazed some of their American counterparts by returning to base with any unused ammunition. The Americans usually preferred to jettison over the jungle, rather than risk a catastrophic explosion in a landing accident. Shown is an English Electric Canberra Mk 20 of No. 2 Squadron, RAAF, flying out of Phan Rang in July 1969. (USAF)
113. Though the F-8 Crusader was designed for supersonic air superiority, the F-8E included a pair of wing racks stressed for 5,000 pounds of external stores. Here an F-8E of Marine Fighter Squadron, All Weather, 312 brings its pair of 2,000lb bombs to bear against Vietcong mortar positions in 1966. (USMC)

114. In March 1968, Lyndon Johnson restricted all bombing operations in North Vietnam to the southern panhandle region. But fighting continued – here an F-105D Thunderchief of the 357th TFS slips away from a KC-135 tanker prior to an April mission. ECM and fuel tanks fill the wing racks, while six 500-pounders are slung beneath the centreline. (USAF)

115. Formal peace talks had begun in Paris in January 1969, and for most of that year North Vietnam was free from US air strikes. This 333rd TFS Republic F-105D Thunderchief carries LAU-3 rocket pods at its outboard wing stations, replacing the ECM pods necessarily carried during missions 'Up North' or into other high threat environments. (USAF)

114▲ 115▼

▲116 ▼117

116. Return of the gun! After experience with externally mounted gun pods on McDonnell Douglas F-4Ds over North Vietnam, the F-4E was introduced with a nose-mounted 20mm Vulcan in 1968. The bombing halt that year restricted air-to-air combat, and the first F-4E gun kill was delayed until May 1972, when a 35th TFS crew nailed a MiG-21. By the war's end, only five more aircraft fell to the F-4Es' cannons. (USAF)
117. Although personal artwork was not as prevalent in Vietnam as in earlier conflicts, it was certainly not non-existent! Here a Wild Weasel crew strategically censors their pin-up while their ground crew and Vietnamese artist look on. (USAF)
118. Over the Mekong River, an 8th TFW McDonnell Douglas F-4D flies along the border between Thailand and Laos in 1969. (Piccirillo)
119. Their bomb racks empty, a pair of Marine Attack Squadron 311 McDonnell Skyhawks return from a 1971 mission. A-4s of the squadron recorded 47,663 combat sorties between June 1965 and May 1971. (USMC)
120. 'Pave Phantom', the RF-4Cs equipped with dorsal 'towelrack' Loran antennas, flew as lead aircraft for several missions in the North. The strike force was usually composed of other F-4s, though Boeing B-52s also bombed using the Loran guided RF-4's instructions. This posed a few problems when the less manoeuvrable B-52s needed last minute course corrections to keep up with the Phantoms. (USAF)

118▲

119▲ 120▼

▲121 ▼122

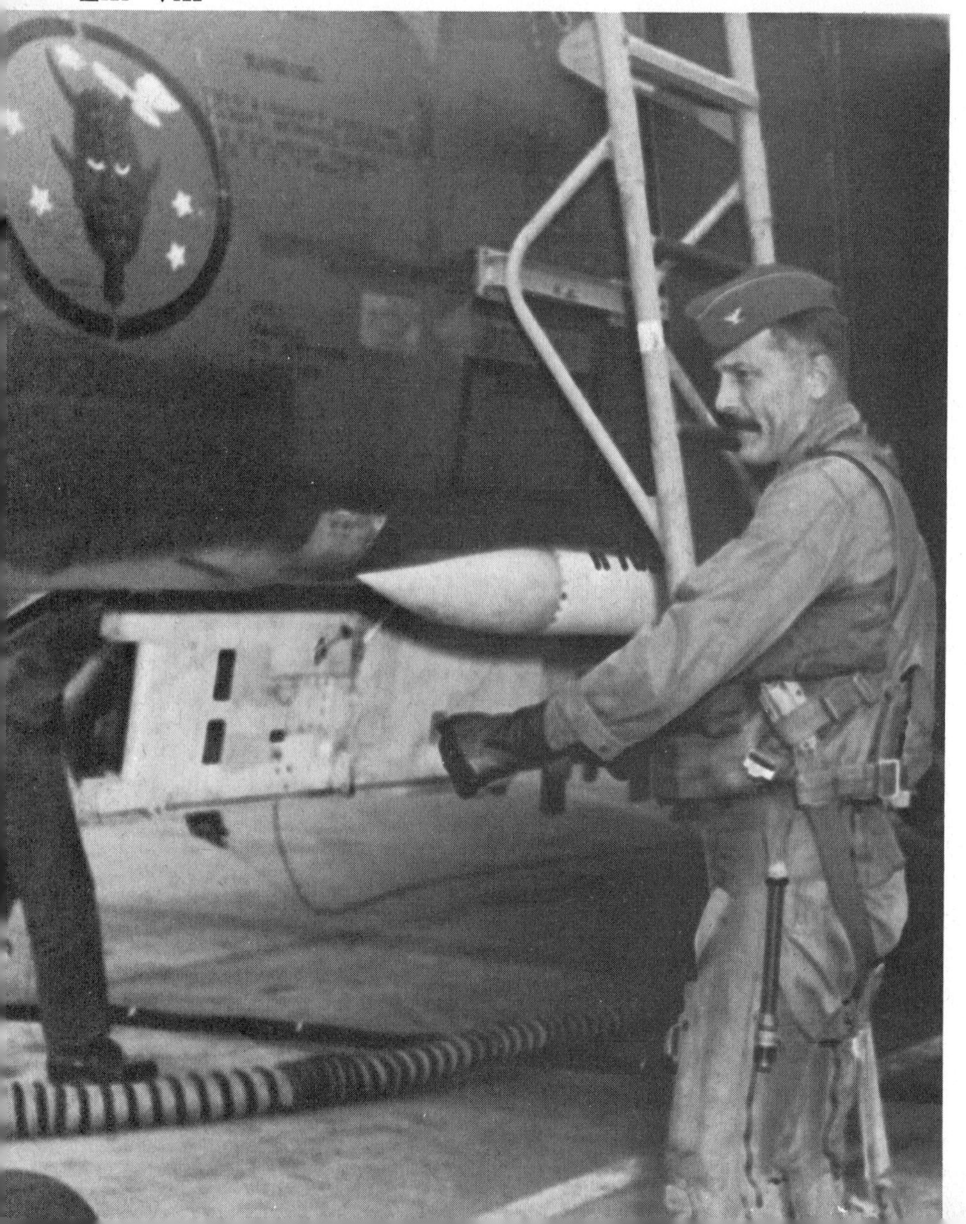

121. An informal ceremony in July 1968 marked the completion of the 100th mission over North Vietnam for five 497th TFS aircrew, and the 200th mission for two others. Although this was a 'dry' ceremony – without benefit of water hoses – the celebrants have inflated their water wing life preservers. Note the leather helmet worn for the occasion, though not for the mission. (Piccirillo)

122. Colonel Robin Olds, commander of the 8th TFW, prepares to board a 433rd TFS Phantom. The squadron's 'Satan's Angels' emblem is on the nose; the tail tip is bright green above the squadron code letters 'FG'. (USAF)

123. Of the 137 MiG kills credited to USAF fliers, a record 39 were accounted for by the 555th TFS. 'Triple Nickle' was assigned first to the 8th TFW (coded 'FY') from March 1966 through May 1968, and then reassigned to the 432nd TRW with code letters 'OY'. (USAF)

124. On temporary duty from the US, a McDonnell Douglas F-4E of the 334th TFS, 4th TFW, carries laser-guided 2,000lb bombs on a mission over North Vietnam. (USAF)

125. Replacing the wing tanks with bombs allowed this 8th TFW F-4D to carry four 2,000lb laser-guided bombs for a limited range. A rendezvous with a KC-135 was essential for any mission up North, but use of a single centreline tank reduced time over target dramatically. (USAF)

123▲

124▲ 125▼

126. A second pair of 8th TFW Phantoms stands off the tanker's wing as a 432nd TFW F-4 takes on fuel. Note the black undersides on the nearest aircraft, assigned to the 'Night Owls' squadron. (USAF)
127. An underside view of a McDonnell Douglas F-4E Phantom with a pair of 2,000lb laser-guided bombs. Sparrows in the two aft bays provide an added measure of air defence, while the two ECM pods in the forward bays passively attempt the same purpose. (USAF)
128. 'Cocked and ready', black-bellied Boeing B-52Ds await their next mission from Anderson AFB, Guam in 1972. In December these aircraft were the backbone of 'Linebacker II', the eleven-day bombing campaign that brought the North Vietnamese back to the negotiating table. (Bishop)

▲126

▲127 ▼128

PART THREE

1. A batch of 2.75in rockets are podded at a hard point on a Douglas B-26; Bien Hoa AB, July 1962. The 'Zuni' rocket pod was a standard armament of US forces in the late 1950s and early 1960s. (USAF)

2. An Army crew unloads a de Havilland C-7A of the 57th Transportation Company (nicknamed Gray Tiger Lines) in October 1966. Within two months all Caribous belonging to the Army would be turned over to the USAF. (USAF)

▲3 ▼4

3. Vietnamese Air Force (VNAF or Veenaff) A-1H Skyraiders fly in support of Vietnamese M-24 light tanks during a training exercise; November 1963. In practice, coordination of air/ground operations usually broke down when the South Vietnamese forces came under attack from the Viet Cong. (USAF)
4. Vietnamese troops help unload an Australian Caribou at Tan Son Nhut in August 1964. This aircraft was one of an initial contingent of three Caribous complete with crews and maintenance personnel sent by the Australian government to aid in the airlift support mission in South Vietnam (USAF)
5. South Vietnamese paratroopers practice handling bundles of air-droppable equipment during training exercises in October 1962. US Air Force Fairchild C-123 Providers supported the operations. (USAF)
6. A US Army de Havilland U-6 Beaver is off-loaded from a Military Air Transport Service C-124 at Bien Hoa in May 1965, ready for the arrival of the first Army combat troops (the 173rd Airborne Brigade) later that month. Fixed-wing Army utility aircraft such as this were needed to facilitate communications. (USAF)

5▲ 6▼

▲7 ▼8

7. Sections of pipe are mounted in the noses of these 500lb fragmentation bombs to force an above-ground explosion, intensifying the deadly effect of the shrapnel. The American instructor pilot was part of the 'Farm Gate' detachment based at Bien Hoa prior to all-out US involvement in the war. (USAF)
8. US Air Force personnel mount front and rear fuzes into fragmentation bombs beneath the wing of a Vietnamese Air Force A-1E Skyraider (USAF)
9. Fuzes are set on 500lb bombs hung beneath a Marine A-4 Skyhawk; September 1965. (USMC)
10. Ejected bomblets stream from underwing canisters as a 531st TFS F-100D Super Sabre makes its run on a Viet Cong base camp; June 1966. (USAF)
11. The commander of the 510th TFS briefs Vietnamese officers on the bomblet dispenser beneath the wing of his North American F-100D; Bien Hoa, May 1967. (USAF)

9▲

10▲ 11▼

▲12 ▼13

12. Members of a six-man team from the 3rd Marines, 9th Marine Expeditionary Brigade run to their Sikorsky CH-34 at the beginning of a reconnaissance patrol; Da Nang, 25 April 1965. (USMC)
13. Army liaison and observation aircraft such as this Cessna O-1D Bird Dog seen at Tan Son Nhut brought not only an aerial method of locating targets but the rudiments of a system of strike coordination; February 1964. (USAF)
14. In 1964 the standard transport of the VNAF was the Douglas C-47 Skytrain. Two squadrons of Skytrains constituted the entire airlift capability of the South Vietnamese Army, until supplemented by surplus US helicopters and USAF transport units. (USAF)
15. USAF activities in Vietnam began with the delivery of defence supplies on transport aircraft. The two heaviest airlifters available in 1964 were the Douglas C-133 Cargomaster and Douglas C-124 Globemaster (background). Although smaller internally than the C-124, the turboprop C-133 could carry up to fourteen tons more payload. (USAF)

14▲ 15▼

◀16

16. Graduation exercises at Nha Trang Air Base, 30 November 1968. A Vietnamese colour guard passes in review as VNAF Cessna U-17s fly overhead. (USAF)
17. During a three-day visit to Saigon, USS *Providence*, flagship of the Seventh Fleet, hosted local dignitaries and delivered more than 38 tons of supplies to humanitarian organizations. The guided missile cruiser's three-hour trip up the Saigon River was escorted by USAF/VNAF air patrols, including this Douglas B-26 Invader; January 1964. (USAF)
18. Accelerated combat activities increased the number of American casualties – an effect that was not lost on the people back home. Flag-draped and bemedalled caskets wait aboard a Fairchild C-123 Provider at the beginning of the long trip to the US. All US Vietnam War dead were identified, making this the first US war not to produce an unknown soldier. (USAF)
19. Static defence – security police at Cam Ranh Bay Air Base chat at a bomb shelter/guard post beside the revetment area; December 1967. This was a new-style sentry post, designed and built by a member of the 12th Security Police Sqn. at the base. (USAF)

17▲ 18▼

19▼

20. Marine air assault – 1966! A door gunner watches from behind his M-60 machine-gun while other Marines sit with their M-14 rifles. (USMC)
21. Sikorsky H-34s were the first major air assault helicopters used by the Vietnamese. This VNAF gunner compares well with his USMC counterpart, though the weapon in this case is an older 30-calibre machine-gun. (USAF)
22. Operation 'Starlite' in August 1965 was the first major USMC combat assault of the war. Three Marine battalions mounted a search and destroy operation south of Chu Lai, killing 623 Viet Cong. A Sikorsky CH-34D is shown delivering ammunition to a Marine howitzer battery on the first day of the attack. (USMC)
23. US Marines dash to a waiting Sikorsky CH-34 as the initial elements take off from the stern of the USS *Iwo Jima.* Travelling light, the Marines completed a series of sea-based assaults during 1965, returning to their ships after each operation. (USMC)

▲20 ▼21

22▲ 23▼

▲24

▲25 ▼26

24. A Republic F-105D Thunderchief of the 23rd TFW at Da Nang in May 1965. The 'Flying Tigers' saw no combat during their temporary duty. Red and white rudder stripes identify the 562nd Tactical Fighter Squadron. (Menard)
25. 'Sylvester the Cat' paints himself orange in response to the motto 'Every Man a Tiger' painted over the left stabilator of F-105D No. 169. (Menard)
26. America's first Christmas in Vietnam; 1964. Members of the 405th Field Maintenance Squadron decorate their tree less than five months after the Tonkin Gulf Resolution brought an open US combat commitment to the Republic of Vietnam. The jets seen here at Tan Son Nhut include Martin B-57 Canberra bombers (black-nosed aircraft at centre), McDonnell RF-101 reconnaissance aircraft (second from left), and General Dynamics F-102 Delta Dagger interceptors (extreme left). (USAF)
27. Major elements of the USAF air rescue team included four A-1 Skyraiders (of the 602nd Special Operations Squadron), a Lockheed HC-130P Hercules (for command and control of the operation and to refuel the rescue helicopter), and a Sikorsky HH-3E Jolly Green Giant. (USAF)
28. An F-4C Phantom of the 'Wolf Pack', the 8th Tactical Fighter Wing, carrying rocket pods over South Vietnam in 1966. (USAF)

27▲ 28▼

▲29 ▼30

31▲

29. A Sikorsky HH-3E (s/n 66-13290) of the 37th Air Rescue Squadron takes off from Da Nang in 1968. (USAF)
30. A Vietnamese Air Force Bell UH-1D gunship moves out of Da Nang between missions. (USAF)
31. A Martin B-57 Canberra rolls to expose its open rotary bomb bay and underwing rocket pods. Fuselage bands and nose tips were red for the 13th Bomb Squadron and medium green for the 8th Bomb Squadron. (USAF)
32. Black smoke pours from the gunpowder cartridge starters on a line-up of Martin B-57s. Canberras of the 8th and 13th Bomb Squadrons were the first jet aircraft assigned to South Vietnam. (USAF)

32▼

▲33 ▼34

35▲

33. The Marines arrive! Taxiing in at Da Nang, these F-4B Phantoms of VMFA-531 (Marine Fighter Attack Squadron 531) represented the first fixed-wing aircraft committed to Vietnam by the USMC; April 1965. (USMC)
34. The flight equipment room of the 13th Bomb Squadron prior to a mission in October 1965. The death's head and 'grim reaper' badge date back to the unit's origins as the 13th Aero Squadron during the Second World War. (USAF)
35. A US Air Force ground crew prepares a 460th Tactical Reconnaissance Wing RF-4C Phantom for a mission over North Vietnam; 1966. The crude pierced steel planking revetments at Tan Son Nhut provided some degree of protection from rocket and mortar attacks until more suitable shelters could be built. (USAF)
36. Kaman HH-43 Huskies operated base rescue and fire-fighting missions under the call-sign 'Pedro'. Fire suppression bottles, boarding ladders, and asbestos-suited firemen were usually dropped just beyond the flaming wreck while the Pedro would advance and beat down the flames with its rotor wash. Note the row of Lockheed SP-2 Neptunes of Patrol Squadron 17 and, behind them, the VNAF C-47 Skytrains (Dakota). (USAF)

36▼

▲37

37. A thin green tail stripe identifies this North American F-100D Super Sabre of the 416th TFS at Bien Hoa in mid-1965. Rows of horizontal bomb symbols, commemorating each mission, are followed by tighter rows of vertical bomb symbols; evidently this 'Hun' saw a good deal more combat than its crew had originally expected! (Menard)
38. 481st TFS North American F-100Ds fly in loose formation over South Vietnam in 1965. The aircraft in the foreground carries napalm bombs on its outboard wing racks. (USAF)
39. Mk. 117 bombs (750-pounders) are prepared for a mission with green-tailed 481st TFS F-100s while Air Force photographers document the effort. (USAF)

▲40

▲41 ▼42

40. A Vietnamese Air Force student pilot completes a lift-off that meets with the approval of his US instructor. The Sikorsky HH-19B Chickasaw carries USAF markings with Vietnamese national insignia. (USAF)
41. An American instructor in the left seat runs through the pre-flight checklist with his student. (USAF)
42. US instructors train Vietnamese student pilots in Sikorsky H-19Bs. The first Vietnamese H-19s, which had come from the French after Dien Bien Phu in 1954, were replaced by ex-USAF aircraft in 1964. Here, a flight practises near the training base at Tan Son Nhut.
43. A Navy Skyraider after coming to grief at Da Nang in early 1966. Attack Squadron 25 operated its A-1s from the aircraft carrier USS *Midway* at 'Yankee Station' in the Gulf of Tonkin. (USAF)
44. VNAF Douglas A-1E and A-1H Skyraiders sit between the sandbag revetments at Bien Hoa as ground crews prepare them for the next mission; January 1966. (USAF)

43▲ 44▼

▲45

45. Intensified combat operations in Vietnam brought a baptism of fire for the USAF's newly operational McDonnell F-4C Phantom. A brief deployment by the 45th TFS in 1965 brought the first two aerial victories for the USAF pilots when two MiG-17s were destroyed on 10 July. Phantom IIs of the 12th TFW, seen here, arrived at Cam Ranh Bay on 8 November 1965 for the first full F-4 wing deployment. (USAF)

46. The second F-4C wing deployed to South-East Asia was the 8th TFW, based at Ubon AB, Thailand in early December 1965. Armament shown is 6×750lb bombs and 4×AIM-7 Sparrows per aircraft. (USAF)

47. During the four-week operation known as 'Birmingham', USAF C-130 Hercules (illustrated) and C-123 Provider aircraft flew almost 1,000 sorties in support of Army brigades near the Cambodian border in Tay Ninh Province. Most of the missions were flown from dirt strips such as this one at Tu Do Not, shown after heavy rains in May 1966. (USAF)

46▲ 47▼

▲48

▲49 ▼50

48. A Douglas EA-1F Skyraider of VAW-13 gets the thumbs-up signal moments before a cat launch from the attack carrier USS *Oriskany* in September 1966. The underwing stores on this aircraft are three fuel tanks and a bulbous electronic countermeasures (ECM) pod for jamming enemy radar. (USN)
49. A Vietnamese A-1E suspended in a rather embarrassing position after a landing accident. (via Menard)
50. Air-mobility formed the basis of US Army strategy in Vietnam and its success depended on the helicopter to provide rapid battlefield movement. But, arguably of equal importance, was the training and spirit of the individual soldier. Here, troopers of the 101st Airborne Division relax near the Cambodian border during Operation 'Pickett' in 1966. The 'hackle' in the gunner's helmet (foreground) is a shaving brush used for cleaning dirt from his M-60 machine-gun. (USAF)
51. First assigned to the Vietnamese 116th Liaison Squadron in 1964, the Cessna U-17A filled a variety of support requirements throughout the war; December 1966. (USAF)
52. Sometimes an FAC likes to be able to shoot back! An Air Force forward air controller adjusts the M-60 machine-gun he has mounted over the rear seat of his Cessna O-1 Bird Dog; May 1966. The success of this one-man, one-gun version of the AC-47 has not been recorded. (USAF)

51▲ 52▼

▲53 ▼54

55▲

53. Strings of 750lb bombs tumble from the bomb bays of a cell of Boeing B-52F Stratofortresses over South Vietnam in 1966. The black-bellied F-models ended their tour in April 1966. (USAF)
54. A 320th Bomb Wing B-52F unloads north-west of Saigon. Fitted with external racks the 'F' could carry 51 bombs, either 500- or 750-pounders. Later modifications to D-model B-52s increased that capacity to a maximum of 108 bombs. (USAF)
55. At Andersen AFB, Guam, CBUs (Cluster Bomb Units) are prepared for a mission. Each of these canisters was designed to break apart over the target, dispersing over a wide area hundreds of smaller anti-personnel bomblets. (USAF)
56. The bomb load from a single B-52 devastates a Viet Cong staging area 30 miles north-east of Saigon in November 1967. Difficulties in locating and identifying enemy strongholds reinforced the impression in the US that the air war was wasted obliterating thousands of Communist-sympathising trees. (USAF)

56▼

◀57 58▲

57. Guided by ground-based radar, a pair of 'BUFFs' (Big Ugly Fat Fellows) or 'Beasts' strike Viet Cong targets in 1967. The B-52D used a three-tone green upper surface camouflage, with gloss black under-surfaces and sides. (USAF)

58. F-105D Thunderchiefs from 355th and 23rd TFW queue on a SAC Boeing KC-135 Stratotanker during refuelling operations in December 1965. (USAF)

59. A pair of 355th TFW Republic F-105Ds carrying their 2,000lb bombs to North Vietnam in December 1965. The unit had begun missions out of Takhli, Thailand only a month before. (USAF)

59▼

▲60 ▼61

60. A Lockheed DC-130 Hercules undergoes an engine change at U-Tapao, Thailand, less than a week before Saigon and the South Vietnamese government fell to the invading North Vietnamese; 24 April 1975. (USAF)
61. By the end of the Vietnam conflict, development of the drone had reached its zenith. The reconnaissance versions of the earlier Ryan Firebees regularly flew over North Vietnam, even when most other aircraft had been ordered to stay south of the 17th Parallel. (USAF)
62. 'Combat Lancer', the deployment of six General Dynamics F-111As from the 428th Tactical Fighter Squadron, began in March 1968. The loss of three aircraft in the next month (in non-combat accidents) overshadowed the combat debut of this controversial aircraft. (USAF)
63. A Vought RF-8A Crusader from Navy Photo Squadron 63 seen here at Da Nang in May 1965. (Menard)

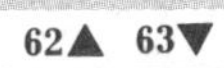
62▲ 63▼

▲64 ▼65

66▲

64. An Air Force Cessna O-1 Forward Air Controller wears International Orange wings and spine for identification and protection from 'friendly' strike aircraft. (USAF)
65. An O-1 Bird Dog wearing VNAF markings. The VNAF mounted their national insignia in all four wing positions. (USAF)
66. An underside view of a Douglas A-1E of the 602nd Fighter Squadron (Commando) covering rescue operations in June 1966. The 602nd had the radio call-sign 'Sandy'. Note the absence of landing gear doors, which was a common feature on USAF and VNAF Skyraiders. (USAF)
67. The Douglas A-1 Skyraider and the US Air Force enjoyed a prolonged love affair from the time the first of the ex-Navy airframes were pressed into service in the early 1960s. The advantages of rugged construction, terrific payload and long loiter time more than excused the type's speed and altitude deficiencies. (USAF)

67▼

U.S. AIR FORCE
USAF

68. A McDonnell Douglas EB-66 Destroyer leads a formation of F-4C Phantoms over the Vietnamese highlands in early 1966. Two of the aircraft conform to new camouflage policies, but five of the Phantoms still wear their original production colours of Light Gull Grey and White. (USAF)

69. Under the guidance of an all-weather Grumman A-6A Intruder, three A-4E Skyhawks of VMA-311 roll in on a target in South Vietnam. (USMC)

70. In 1965 the drone was brought to Vietnam as a remote-controlled target for ground-based anti-aircraft batteries. This Ryan BQM-34 Firebee is mounted beneath the wing of a Lockheed DP-2E; Da Nang Air Base, November 1965. (USN)

71. Information on the Air Force's drone reconnaissance programme during the Vietnam War is only now surfacing. In one of the earliest known photographs of reconnaissance versions of Ryan BQM-34s in South-East Asia, a Lockheed DC-130A is seen landing at Pha Binh Dien in March 1966. (USAF)

69▲

70▲ 71▼

◀68

▲72 ▼73

72. A smooth black Martin RB-57E at Tan Son Nhut in December 1965; the excellent condition of the finish would indicate a recent repainting. (USAF)
73. Several months later and the same airframe is well patched. Hundreds of shrapnel holes were inflicted during a mortar attack on 13/14 April 1966. (USAF)
74. A Vought F-8E Crusader of Marine All Weather Fighter Squadron 232 taxis for take-off at Da Nang; March 1967. The 'Red Devils' began combat operations in December 1966. (USMC)
75. The low-altitude parachute extraction system (LAPES) was developed to deliver cargo precisely without having to land the transport aircraft. As this TAC C-130E skims the airstrip at An Khe, a parachute opens and the Hercules flies from its palletized load; June 1966. (USAF)
76. Declared surplus to USAF requirements, the Fairchild C-123 Provider was scheduled to be phased out of the USAF inventory in 1961. But, just as Secretary of Defense Robert McNamara suggested turning the aircraft over to the Army, the Air Force recognized new requirements for the type. Although weighing twice as much as the Caribou, the Provider still had exceptional rough field/short field characteristics. This 311th Air Commando Squadron C-123 slips onto the grass strip at Gia Vuc under the watchful eye of an Army Special Forces controller. (USAF)

74▲

75▲ 76▼

▲77 ▼78

79▲

77. Army troops relax during Operation 'Attleboro' – a battle mounted against four Viet Cong and North Vietnamese regiments in central Tay Ninh Province – as a de Havilland CV-2A Caribou (later redesignated C-7A) lifts off from a rough landing strip in November 1966. (USAF)
78. This photograph shows a CV-2A Caribou of the Army's 61st Aviation Company on a mission over South Vietnam in September 1966. (USAF)
79. By 1966, the Army had agreed to turn over its CV-2 Caribous to the US Air Force, ending an ongoing dispute over the control of airlift operations. At Vung Tan, an Air Force crew checks out in the de Havilland. In the 1980s, as the Air Force prepares to retire its last C-7A (CV-2 redesignation) unit, there is again talk of the Army regaining its valued transports. (USAF)
80. De Havilland Caribous were the most effective light transports in the theatre. First introduced to Vietnam by US Army advisers in August 1961, the Caribou's short field capabilities were unparalleled. This aircraft was part of the Australian contingent in 1966. (USAF)
81. Wearing Army camouflage and Air Force markings, a CV-2 drops in at the Special Forces camp at Ha Thanh; 23 June 1969. (USAF)

80▲ 81▼

▲82

82. At 00.20 hours on 15 July 1967, the Viet Cong attacked Da Nang AB with rockets and mortars, destroying 10 aircraft and damaging 49 others. The force of the blast in the top revetment blew down the rear wall, destroyed the adjacent aircraft and flipped its tail into the third revetment. At far right in the photograph is the burned-out hulk of a Lockheed C-130A Hercules. (USAF)

83. 'Skoshi Tiger' was the operation that evaluated Northrop's bantamweight F-5 in combat in South-East Asia. The aircraft in the foreground, with an external refuelling probe, was designated an F-5C, while the other two aircraft were shorter-ranged F-5As. (USAF)

84. An early response to the threat from surface-to-air missiles was the deployment of Shrike missiles (AGM-45), carried by special teams known as 'Wild Weasels'. One Weasel would probe the North Vietnamese 'Fan Song' radar defence, provoking a response that would reveal the position of the SAMs, giving other members of the team an opportunity to destroy the facility. The Shrike-armed aircraft shown here is an F-105 Thunderchief. (USAF)

83▲ 84▼

MILITARY AIR TRANSPORT SERVICE
U.S. AIR FORCE
THÔNG BÁO
ĐÂY KHU VỰC HẠN CHẾ
WARNIN
RESTRICTED A
IT IS UNLAWFUL TO ENTER
AREA WITHOUT WRITTEN PER
OF THE USAF CMDR. DANA

▲85

06073

▲86 ▼87

24483
TG-483
U.S. AIR FORCE

88▲

85. The USAF's first jet transports were 15 C-135As and 30 C-135Bs of the Military Air Transport Service. The aircraft illustrated is a Boeing C-135B of the 438th Military Airlift Wing, MAC, at Da Nang in 1966. (USAF)
86. A small number of Cessna U-3A 'Blue Canoes' served with the Pacific Air Forces in Vietnam as liaison aircraft for staff level personnel; Tan Son Nhut, May 1967. (USAF)
87. The Cessna U-3s were supplemented by twin-jet North American T-39 Sabreliners; December 1967. (USAF)
88. US Senator Barry Goldwater was the Republican Party's presidential candidate in 1964. Labelled a warmonger during the election, he lost to the encumbent Lyndon Johnson. Whatever course the war would have taken with Goldwater as President, most agree that US policies would have been different! The Senator is seen here in a Huey during a tour of South Vietnam in 1969. (USAF)
89. South Vietnamese Premier Nguyen Cao Ky (right), members of his staff, and US Ambassador Elsworth Bunker (left) inspect a VNAF Sikorsky H-34 during ceremonies at Bien Hoa in June 1967. (USAF)

89▼

▲90 ▼91

90. A Marine Boeing-Vertol CH-46 Sea Knight lifts a 90ft pole at Da Nang during the construction of a new tactical air control centre (TACC) on nearby Monkey Mountain. Operational in 1966, the Monkey Mountain facility controlled the air defence of northern South Vietnam and aided operations over North Vietnam and the Gulf of Tonkin. (USAF)

91. The recovery of downed aircraft saved millions of dollars in replacement planes and parts. The replacement value of this CH-34, being carried by a Sikorsky piston-engined CH-37 after action near Da Nang in October 1965, was roughly a quarter of a million dollars. (USAF)

92. Photographs of wounded aircrew and the damaged aircraft they flew home safely were far more common during the Second World War, partly because the complex systems of modern jets could be dealt a fatal blow more readily than their counterparts of the 1940s. Nevertheless, when 87 pieces of North Vietnamese shrapnel took out the electrical system of Captain B. R. Reinbold's F-105 Thunderchief and wounded Reinbold, the aircraft and pilot returned safely to base; August 1966. (USAF)

93. An Air Force McDonnell Douglas RF-101 Voodoo pilot brought home this remarkable photograph of a North Vietnamese 57mm gun and crew in action. The reconnaissance aircraft is already passing the battery as the muzzle of the 57mm erupts with rounds that can only miss. (USAF)

92▲ 93▼

▲94

▲95 ▼96

97▲ 98▼

94. Units of Air Force fire-fighting equipment shine in the hazy sun at Pleiku Air Base in July 1966. (USAF)
95. The 1st Air Cav (1st Cavalry Division, Airborne) designated several of its helicopters for command and control of assault missions. This Bell UH-1 mounts additional radio antennae along the rear boom and target-marking rockets below the cabin, while inside an Air Force forward air controller coordinates air strikes. (USAF)
96. An Army UH-1B 'Hog' (as Huey gunships were nicknamed) is refuelled in the field; October 1965. This 6th Cavalry helicopter mounts fixed 2.75in rocket pods and movable 7.62mm machine-guns. Note the pilot's gunsight inside the cockpit. (USAF)
97. The first Vietnam deployment of the Marines' heavy-lift Sikorsky CH-53A brought four aircraft from HMH-463 to Marble Mountain Air Facility in early 1967. By the time they were joined by the remainder of their unit that May, the original four Sea Stallions had recovered 103 damaged aircraft! (USAF)
98. Air Force Vice Chief of Staff General William Blanchard, Seventh Air Force Commander Lieutenant General Joseph Moore, and base commander Colonel Levi Chase (back to camera) observe construction activities during the expansion of Cam Ranh Bay Air Base in April 1966. The increase in air activity over Vietnam brought a massive enlargement of all Vietnam bases – on both sides of the Demilitarized Zone! (USAF)

▲99 ▼100

99. 'The White Whale' was a Fairchild C-123 Provider used to transport press staff and coordinate military news activities. (USAF)
100. Green Jolly Green! The first Sikorsky CH-3Cs sent to South-East Asia were camouflaged overall with dark-green paint. The colour was briefly used at the same time that American television began advertising 'Green Giant' brand vegetables ('. . . Good things from the Valley of the Jolly Green Giant . . .') and the name was snapped up by crews. (USAF)

101. 'Deuces' on a combat air patrol (CAP) over South Vietnam in 1966. General Dynamics F-102A Delta Daggers served long but uneventfully, never seeing combat! (USAF)
102. The container delivery system (CDS) allowed cargo drops at an altitude of 600ft rather than 1,000ft, keeping supplies from scattering over a wide area. Barely visible against the ground terrain, a 309th TAS Fairchild C-123 Provider climbs to drop its cargo at the Dak Pek Special Forces camp, April 1970. (USAF)

101▲ 102▼

▲103 ▼104

103. A Royal Thai Air Force C-123 Provider lands at the American Special Forces camp on Phu Quoc Island; November 1966. Located in the Gulf of Thailand, off the Cambodian/South Vietnamese border, the facility doubled as a training camp for the Army of the Republic of Vietnam (ARVN). (USAF)
104. In September 1966, five battalions of the 101st Airborne Division initiated Operation 'Thayer I', a pursuit of North Vietnamese troops from the plains of Binh Dinh to the Cay Giep Mountains. Here, members of the two battalions jumping off from landing zone 'Hammond' wait by a USAF C-123 Provider as an Army UH-1D approaches. (USAF)
105. In addition to the transport aircraft of the various military services, commercial transport aircraft delivered a large proportion of the civil and military supplies and personnel that flooded into Vietnam during the war years. A Pan American Boeing 707 is here unloaded and refuelled at Tan Son Nhut Air Base near Saigon in November 1966. (USAF)
106. During construction at Tuy Hoa Air Base in August 1966, an Alaska Airways 'Golden Nugget Freighter' unloads supplies across the ramp from its military cousins – Lockheed C-130 Hercules. (USAF)
107. USAF personnel arrive at Da Nang in June 1969. Braniff was one of several commercial airlines that operated flights to Vietnam's major airports. (USAF)

105▲

106▲ 107▼

U.S. ARMY
UH-1D
U.S.A. SERIAL
498TH
CARGO HOOK
MAX LOAD
EXIT RELEASE

▲108 ▼109

SS
952

108. An Air Force cameraman records an Army UH-1D medevac helicopter lifting off near Kontum during Operation 'Pickett' in 1966. (USAF)
109. A North American F-100D Super Sabre of the 309th TFS, 31st TFW, glides over the beach road on its final approach to Tuy Hoa. (M. L. Cross, Jr.)
110. The Douglas AC-47's gunsight was mounted at the pilot's left shoulder. (USAF)
111. Damaged in a collision with a North American OV-10 Bronco, this Douglas AC-47 gunship crash-landed at Bien Hoa on 14 December 1968. (USAF)

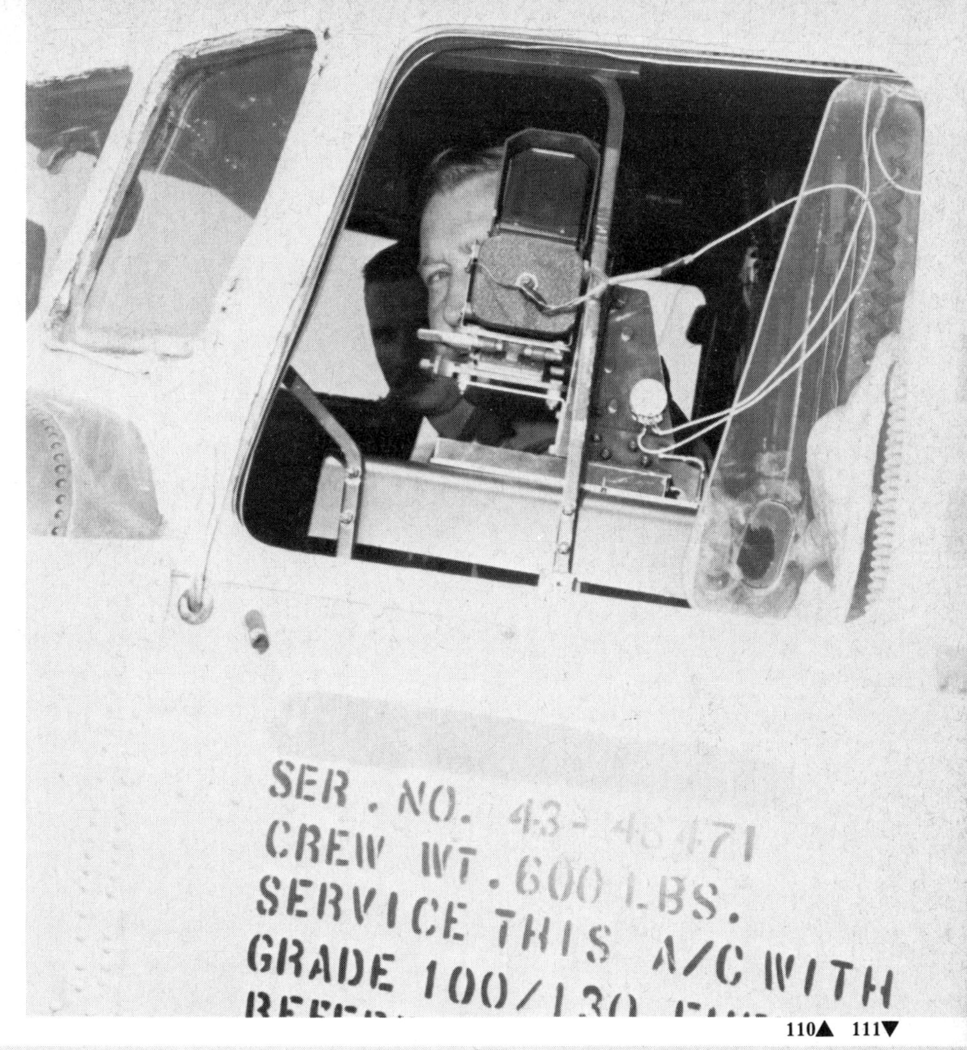

110▲ 111▼

▲112

112. A pair of AC-47 gunships silhouetted by the sunset at Pleiku Air Base; 1966. (USAF)
113. May 1967 and the amphibious assault ship USS *Tripoli* (LPH-10) departs Pearl Harbor with Marine Heavy Helicopter Squadron 463 and elements of Marine Observation Squadron 6, bound for Vietnam. As flagship of Amphibious Ready Group 'Bravo'/TG 76.5, *Tripoli* participated in eight amphibious operations by the end of the year. (USMC)
114. An Air Force C-141 Starlifter pilot of the 3rd Military Airlift Squadron, seen during deployment of the 101st Airborne Division to Vietnam in 1967. (The crash helmet, which was designed for transport crews, proved unpopular and was soon dropped from use.) (USAF)
115. A Marine F-4B Phantom lands aboard the USS *Enterprise* after operations in January 1975. Restricted from combat operations by a Congressional mandate, American forces remained hours from Vietnam as Communist troops scored victory after victory. (USAF)

▼113

114▲ 115▼

116. A Marine CH-46 lands with a maintenance crew and the spare parts to repair a C-130 Hercules transport of the 345th TAS damaged by ground fire; An Hoa Airfield, March 1969. (USAF)
117. An Army 105mm howitzer is hooked to an Air Force CH-3C during Operation 'Mastif' in March 1966. Cooperation at this level was not often necessary, as Army heavy-lift helicopters were usually available to support ground operations. (USAF)

116▼ 117▲

▲118

118. Seats on military airlifters are about as comfortable as those on older airliners, though the removable Air Force seats face rearward for safety. The 101st had to do without stewardesses and in-flight films, but the trip was still more comfortable than in a canvas webbed rack; December 1967. (USAF)

119. There are jokes about the quartermasters who issue snow parkas to troops bound for the jungle, but during 'Eagle Thrust' those quartermasters would have earned medals. The airlift route followed a great loop through Alaska, including a stop-over in a snowstorm! Here, a Lockheed C-141 is de-iced before continuing the mission. (USAF)

120. Safe in warmer climes, troopers of the 101st are led from their C-141 Starlifter at Bien Hoa. A month later, most of these men would be helping to crush the Viet Cong's Tet Offensive of January 1968. (USAF)

119▲ 120▼

▲121 ▼122

121. An American infantryman directs a UH-1D to a landing zone at Kontum near the Cambodian border during Operation 'Pickett' in 1966. (USAF)

122. An armed Huey approaches a soldier and smoke marker to evacuate wounded soldiers; October 1966. (USAF)

123▲

124▲ 125▼

123. Propaganda leaflets drop from a 4th Special Operations Wing Cessna O-2B on a psy-war mission. A peaceful and beautiful countryside below often belied guerrilla, political and military activities. The belly of this 'Super Skymaster' has a special gloss black paint to counter the effects of exhaust and oil stains. (USAF)
124. An early camouflage applied to a Douglas A-1H of the Vietnamese 83rd Fighter Squadron; Da Nang Air Base, May 1965. (Menard)
125. A Lockheed SP-2H of Navy Patrol Squadron 1 searches for suspicious vessels in the coastal waters of South Vietnam. (USN)

▲126

126. Operation 'Eagle Thrust' became the longest and largest military airlift into a combat zone. In December 1967, the 'Screaming Eagles' of the 101st Airborne Division moved from Fort Campbell, Kentucky to Vietnam. (The first brigade had been in Vietnam since 1965.) A total of 369 C-141 missions and 22 C-133 missions were needed to move 10,024 troops and 5,300 tons of equipment. Here, the division's Hueys are prepared for the journey. (USAF)

127. An Air Force O-1E Bird Dog flies in over a U-10 and a CH-47 Chinook to land at Plei Djereng Special Forces Camp in the Vietnamese highlands; November 1966. (USAF)

128. The only photograph of a Medal of Honor action in progress. In the final moments of Kham Duc's service as a Special Forces camp, Lieutenant Colonel Joe M. Jackson landed to pick up three survivors, seen running to Jackson's C-123 at the centre of the runway. Most of the camp was already in enemy hands as Jackson turned and took off under fire. A crashed C-130 Hercules and Cessna O-2 are visible at the lower left of the photograph; May 1968. (USAF)

▼127

128▶

▲129

129. Rocket pods and 7.62mm miniguns supplement the internal 20mm cannon of this pair of Navy OV-10 Broncos from Light Attack Squadron 4; Mekong Delta, June 1969. (USN)

130. The North American OV-10 Bronco was one of the few effective multi-service aircraft developed during Robert McNamara's tenure as Secretary of Defense. First designed for counter-insurgency, the turboprop Bronco was expected to be the answer to most needs in a brushfire war such as Vietnam. Here, a Marine OV-10A rolls in on a target during a 1970 FAC mission near Da Nang. (USMC)

▼130